Praise for
Count It All Joy:
Life's Lessons from a Child with Special Needs

"An emotionally raw disclosure of the untold truths of love, patience, personal growth and family success behind raising a child with Down syndrome. An expertly articulated message of hope and courage not only for families with special needs children, but an enlightened message for all. A humbling, remarkable read."

—S. Jasmine Demos DNP, CRNP
Adult/Pediatric Nurse Practitioner
Doctor of Nursing Practice

"Honest, inspiring, informative, loving, and most importantly, hopeful, especially for parents facing life with a special needs child. Loved it!"

—Sue Stiles, BS
Special Education Teaching Assistant

"A beautiful, loving tribute to a son and to all children who learn differently … reminds us to cherish the greatest gifts which don't always come in expected packages."

—Michele Savant, MS
Special Education Teacher

"Count It All Joy is a must read for every parent of a special needs child. Dr. Murray's frank portrayal of her anxieties and challenges regarding her son is a reality for many parents who have a child with special needs and the hopelessness we often face on a daily basis. Dr. Murray offers a positive response to life's challenges."

—Christine Pullen
Parent of a child with autism

"A wonderful, candid, heart-felt portrayal of raising a child with Down syndrome and autism. This book will encourage all of us to open our hearts to the beauty and blessings of children with special needs."

—Kim Matthews, MSW
Social Worker

COUNT
IT ALL
Joy

Life's Lessons from a Child
with Special Needs

KATHLEEN MURRAY, PhD

WESTBOW
PRESS®
A DIVISION OF THOMAS NELSON
& ZONDERVAN

This book is a work of non-fiction. Unless otherwise noted, the author
and the publisher make no explicit guarantees as to the accuracy of
the information contained in this book and in some cases, names of
people and places have been altered to protect their privacy.

Scripture quotations come from the Catholic Women's
Devotional Bible, New Revised Standard Version. Copyright
© 2000 by Zondervan. All rights reserved.

This title is also available as a WestBow Press ebook.
Visit www.westbowpress.com/ebooks.

Author Photo by Photography by Scott Pfeiffer
www.pfeiffer-photo.com

WestBow Press books may be ordered through booksellers or by contacting:

WestBow Press
A Division of Thomas Nelson & Zondervan
1663 Liberty Drive
Bloomington, IN 47403
www.westbowpress.com
1 (866) 928-1240

Because of the dynamic nature of the Internet, any web addresses or
links contained in this book may have changed since publication and
may no longer be valid. The views expressed in this work are solely those
of the author and do not necessarily reflect the views of the publisher,
and the publisher hereby disclaims any responsibility for them.

Any people depicted in stock imagery provided by Thinkstock are
models, and such images are being used for illustrative purposes only.
Certain stock imagery © Thinkstock.

ISBN: 978-1-5127-0682-6 (sc)
ISBN: 978-1-5127-0683-3 (hc)
ISBN: 978-1-5127-0681-9 (e)

Library of Congress Control Number: 2015912657

Print information available on the last page.

WestBow Press rev. date: 10/01/2015

CONTENTS

DEDICATION

To those who have been blessed to know and love a person with Down syndrome and to those who have not yet been so blessed.

To my sweet son, Christian, who has inspired me to
become a better person and have a deeper relationship
with our Savior, Jesus Christ, and our glorious God.

To Matt and Amanda, for embracing the
special qualities in Christian,
offering unconditional love to him and
for providing years of happiness
to our family.

And to my husband, Dave, for his love
and support and for providing
strength and wisdom beyond compare. For encouraging me to
share our story so that other parents may
seek joy each and every day
with their children and with each other.

My grace is sufficient for you, for power is made perfect in weakness.

—2 Corinthians 12:9

PREFACE

When our son, Christian, was born in 2001, there was scant literature about the daily life experiences of a child with Down syndrome. I was, however, provided with books containing definitions of Trisomy 21 (the medical term for Down syndrome), medical facts and statistics, and expected negative outcomes for such a child's physical, educational, and behavioral characteristics. I read those books diligently and began formulating a laundry list of everything I could expect to go wrong with Christian as he grew.

Within a year of his birth, Christian had open heart surgery to repair a serious birth defect, and within four years, our suspicions that he had autism, in addition to Down syndrome, were confirmed. Transitioning from a place of anxiety and despair to a place of joy and peace, embracing challenges with a positive attitude, and providing unconditional love for Christian were conscious decisions revisited frequently.

This book is my testimony, my personal account of the beauty and uniqueness of a child with special needs and an account of how raising this child has blessed me. My testimony is that Christian has taught life lessons to me that I may not have learned had it not been for what many consider his disabilities.

Let me confess that I started with neither an open heart nor an open mind to embrace the miracle and blessing of Christian from the very first moment of his life. This was mostly because the prospect wasn't presented to me as an option. Over the years, I have realized that I wasted precious moments in negativity and wish fervently that I had been told of the amazing future that I could have with Christian. But Christian taught me those lessons on a daily basis.

Parents of a child with special needs struggle, just as they would with a typical child; that's what parenting is all about. We are all aware that no child is given a struggle-free life card along with his/her birth certificate, and there is no choice in this matter. However, each of us has a choice as to how we think and feel about the experiences we will have with our child. The following anecdotes are testimony of my transformation from hopelessness and negativity to beauty, hope, and joy.

Here am I, the servant of the Lord; let it be with me according to your word.

—Luke 1:38

LESSON 1

TODAY

Today is the day I decided to write about life with Christian, our now thirteen-year-old son with Down syndrome and autism.

What makes an eighteen-foot Slip-N-Slide the center of the universe to Christian? He intently watches glistening water droplets bounce off the sea-blue landing strip, with neck craned, arms extended, face gleaming upward, and eyes squinted, reveling in the streams of water splashing against his remarkably long tongue. There are many ways to be fully immersed in this simple activity, and Christian found all of them.

My limited mind never imagined any but the usual ways to use this simple toy, but Christian jumped on the slide and created playful melodies of water, streaming like a symphony. Such joy to watch him, belly down, back arched, arms extended across the slide and racing back to the start for endless encores. Then there were Christian's precision bounces, with just the right pressure to squirt water rivulets in rhythmic succession from the openings in the supply tubing. Forward, backward, sideways across the slide into the reservoir. Pure joy! From a distance, I can feel his joy. I feel it enter my soul and warm me from the inside, and I feel a gentle smile pull the corners of my lips upward toward the heavens. And I feel joy in the moment, along with him.

I didn't feel this joy when I began my journey with Christian. I wish I had. I was always told by the experts and caring friends, who, with a pacifying voice, said, "It's going to be okay," after Christian was born. These well-meaning people might make the same remark to a friend after the death of a loved one. But now, I am telling my stories of discovery for parents of a child with special needs, and I say, "It's not going to be okay; it's going to be *better* than okay—much, much better!"

Don't settle for anything less. Find the beauty in your child. Live in the fullness of your child and create beauty for your future today.

Cast all your anxiety on him, because he cares for you.

—1 Peter 5:7

LESSON 2

WORRY

"Don't worry; he won't have Down syndrome." Family, friends, neighbors, and strangers all said some variation of these words when I was pregnant. After the first ultrasound, a heart specialist reported, "The heart defect is a certainty, but we can fix the heart. However, Down syndrome is associated with this type of heart defect, and we can't fix that. Don't worry, though; he may not have that." What a difference it would've made if I could have heard, "He might have Down syndrome, and your life with him will be full and joyful. He will be beautiful and do things that will drive you crazy, like all kids do. He will be sweet and special and bless your life beyond your wildest dreams." If only I could have heard *that*.

Today, if God said to me, "I will allow you to go back to Christian's birth, and I will remove either the heart defect or Down syndrome. You choose which one." Without hesitation, I would respond, "God, I choose for You to fix his heart, but don't fix Down syndrome. Don't fix that." Don't worry.

For my thoughts are not your thoughts, nor are your ways my ways, says the Lord. For as the heavens are higher than the earth, so are my ways higher than your ways and my thoughts than your thoughts.

—Isaiah 55:8–9

DOORS

My emotional doors slammed shut as soon as Christian was born, and my fears were confirmed. The doctors bowed their heads and averted their eyes from mine, stating, "He has Down syndrome." But there he was—an infant, cooing and drooling as he looked into my eyes. But behind my doors, bitterness was oozing, barring all the possibilities for our new baby. Negative thoughts rang over and over in my head: *He won't go to college; he won't drive; he won't marry; he won't be the star of the football team. He won't, he won't, he won't.* Attempts to change my focus were futile and became, *He will pack groceries; he will stuff envelopes; he will wipe tables. He will, he will, he will.* Words tortured me. Words blinded me to his precious innocence and all the potential and promise for an amazing future. So limited was my thinking.

Christian's doors hold promise, unique experiences, and happiness with every door he opens. His bedroom door opens, and he peeks out, looking for someone to take him downstairs for breakfast. The bus door opens, swinging outward and welcoming Christian for an adventurous field trip. The classroom door opens, with a team of teachers and therapists greeting him daily, with skills and activities to help him learn. The church doors open, and Christian seeks out his usual spot in the back row to provide a non-verbal salutation to all entering parishioners. Restaurant doors open for a fun night out to enjoy our favorite cuisine. Mentally, I imagined only closed doors for Christian, and he wasn't even old enough to open any. It's better to keep our hearts and minds unbound—a wonderful experience may occur if we're willing to simply open the door.

Ask, and it will be given to you; search, and you will find; knock, and the door will be opened for you.

—Matthew 7:7

LESSON 4

LOCKS

Locks, I thought, would be everywhere in our house. In my mind, I heard and believed *I'll have to watch him every minute of every day. I'll never get a break. He's never going to be safe out of my sight.* That panic, turning to resentment, set in for situations that hadn't even happened but that I expected would come.

Over the years, my husband, Dave, and I have tried to stay one step ahead of Christian. We are aware that his safety awareness is limited and that he doesn't always remember safety instructions, despite repetition. So we reversed the lock on his bedroom door and moved the latch from the inside to the outside of the gate, well out of his reach. We added child-proof door devices on all inside doors. We placed noise makers for movement throughout the house. We pulled the burner knobs off the stove every time we cooked. *Surely that would do it*, or so we thought.

In late June a few years back, in my typically diligent survey of the backyard, I momentarily couldn't see Christian. Knowing that we had secured the premises, I calmly rounded the corner of the far end of the house to find that he had tried to climb over the locked gate and was hanging from the fence post by his shorts, safely suspended on the correct side of the fence. I carefully removed him from the post, and he steadfastly pointed to his favorite tree in the neighbor's yard. As I opened the gate, Christian hurriedly ran and stopped at the base of the tree, looking up, watching, and listening. He was fascinated by the rustling leaves swaying in the breeze—beautiful sights and sounds.

Christian wants the world accessible. He will show us things we might miss. It's a constant compromise for independence and safety. Combining freedom and protection can be tricky. Security is never guaranteed despite the best locks.

I praise you, for I am fearfully and wonderfully made.

—Psalm 139:14

LESSON 5

EARS

Can't they pin those ears up? How they flop over and curl downward. If you look at him from the back, you can really tell there's something wrong with him. All those thoughts I had soon after his birth. Staring at him through the enclosed bassinet in the pediatric intensive care unit of the hospital, I disappointedly stared at those ears, already limiting his potential and mine for a normal life, as I envisioned it. Turning away, I shed tears for dreams shattered.

Children with Down syndrome are prone to middle ear infections that can limit hearing, so Christian's hearing ability in his early years was a big concern. We clapped our hands together loudly and startled him with various noises to be sure his ears were working, and he turned (albeit slowly) toward the sound with curiosity. Just as we were checking hearing off the list of impairments associated with Down syndrome, a hearing test and a test for middle ear fluid showed he needed PE tubes (pressure equalization tubes) to help drain his ears and to help him hear better. We made many trips to the doctor's office, resulting in minor surgery for drainage tubes. Meanwhile, we practiced having Christian look at us when we spoke to him and made sure to be close to him when we were talking and showing him what to do. His ears received all kinds of sounds, and he was curious about all the noises inside and outside of our house. After the third insertion of the tubes, and again, finding the tiny, clear tubes that fell out of his ears throughout the house again and again, the doctor told us Christian didn't need to have them reinserted and that his hearing was pretty close to normal. Good news and one more specialist to check off our list.

As I fast-forward to the present time, Christian's dad and I, together, nestle those soft ears against our cheeks, giving us utter delight. I see Christian's older brother, Matt, and younger sister, Amanda, gently and lovingly flick those adorable ears, with giggles from all—especially Christian. I see my hands cup those precious ears in the bitter-cold Chicago air as I slowly exhale warm air in a smooth *haaaa* at Christian's request for the game he calls "Do *haaaa*," while we wait for the school bus.

Playing the *whisper game* in Christian's ears is also hilarious. It goes like this. First, you encircle his ear with your hands and whisper gibberish into it. Then he looks up at you, surprised, with his head tilted sideways, as he says in a high-pitched voice, "Really?" Then he takes his turn whispering gibberish into your ear, and you, in turn, respond in falsetto, "Really?" My thoughts have never returned to negativity over the sight of those floppy ears.

Let your adornment be the inner self with the lasting beauty of a gentle and quiet spirit, which is very precious in God's sight.

—1 Peter 3:4

LESSON 6

EYES

Squinting, bulging eyes, the fat folds of skin, the wide spacing of his eyes, his eyeball movement side to side called *nystagmus* (a ridiculous word) were all apparent in Christian. I have guilty memories of how I disliked those eyes when Christian was first placed in my arms. How I cursed those squinted eyes when he was born. I wondered if he could even see me. Would he recognize me? Would he ever be able to make sense of anything in print? I was drowning in negativity as I turned away and refused to look into those eyes. Lost moments that I cannot regain.

A specialist confirmed a *visual deficit* and recommended eyeglasses for Christian when he was in elementary school. However, eyeglasses were not on Christian's list of comfortable accessories. It shouldn't have surprised us that Christian wouldn't wear glasses. Because of his sensory deficits, Christian detested anything touching his face or his head. Hats, swim goggles, and washcloths to wipe the spaghetti dinner off his cheeks and forehead would send Christian into a tizzy when he was younger. Over time, he slowly tolerated a winter hat, because it wasn't nearly as bad as the frigid Chicago winter air. He also eventually allowed us to do a quick swipe of his face with a washcloth after meals.

Although Christian looked extremely cute and stylish in his glasses, and we praised him each time he put them on, after a few seconds, he would apologetically tilt his head down, remove the glasses, and hand them to us. Over the course of a year, with numerous, yet futile incentives, we tried to get Christian to wear his glasses.

After several discussions, we decided that since he navigated his environment with fairly good precision and could read slightly enlarged print, we would forego the glasses. Placing Christian on the left side of the room helped optimize his *null* point (where objects did not appear to shake) and helped him to see things at a distance a little better. The glasses might've been beneficial to Christian, but the scale tipped in favor of him not wearing them. Sometimes you can't get your kids to do what's best for them, despite your urging and prodding; and if it doesn't involve the loss of life or limb, you just have to settle for mediocrity. Christian's eyes work well enough for him to meet his needs at the moment.

I now treasure countless times of falling in love with those eyes and the person behind them. Beautiful eyes. No maliciousness, no spite, no deceitful intent in those eyes. Eyes that can read his favorite night-time story book, *God Made Me Special.* Eyes that will stare into your eyes with peacefulness for as long as you want to gaze at him. Tender, innocent, loving eyes.

Whatever is true, whatever is honorable, whatever is just, whatever is pure, whatever is pleasing, whatever is commendable, if there is any excellence and if there is anything worthy of praise, think about these things.

—Philippians 4:8

HEART

The card sitting next to Christian on the hearth was larger and taller than he stood at age seven. The card was plastered with a multitude of cut-out paper hearts, glued to the four-foot-tall card, each red heart personally signed.

"Who is that person, the name on the heart in the corner? A neighbor we barely know?" I asked.

My husband replied, "Yes, he heard about Christian. His blood type matched Christian's and he wanted to help. Three other neighbors provided their blood for Christian too."

Christian's surgery was three months away, the second of two open-heart surgeries. We took a trip back to Baltimore to see family and friends, just in case the surgery didn't go well.

Christian survived both surgeries, and we are so grateful. The love and support we received from both near and far overwhelmed us. A gift basket was waiting for us when we returned from the hospital. It was so large that we had to bring it in sideways from the garage. Prayers, gift cards, toys, and food came to us, reminding us that Christian is valued and loved. Each day since his surgery, we're reminded that coursing through Christian's heart is the blood of some of our wonderful neighbors. To give a part of oneself for another's life is so precious a gift.

Christian's heart is not fixed because his valves still leak, according to the cardiologist, and he continues to see this specialist on a yearly basis. Christian cannot be exposed to extreme hot or cold temperatures for extended periods. Because of this, Christian was assigned to one of a few air-conditioned elementary schools in our district and to an air-conditioned bus to take him to school (a little perk).

He cannot exert himself physically to intense levels. Consequently, a special aide was assigned at school to help him regulate his activity (i.e., rest often), as he would chase, jump, and play wildly until he became over-excited and exhausted. He might need additional heart surgeries as he grows, and we have been told that his life expectancy is shorter than his same-aged peers. There is a saying that goes, "It's what's on the inside that counts." I think that saying can mean that the heart of a person is their soul and the content of their being. For the time that Christian is here with us, I want to experience his affectionate, sweet, tender heart.

Do not judge, so that you may not be judged. For the judgment you make you will be judged, and the measure you give will be the measure you get.

—Matthew 7:1–2

L E S S O N 8

MIRRORS

I often wondered over the years what Christian sees when he looks at himself in the mirror. As many infants do, Christian had a mirror attached to the side of his crib, facing inward, so that he could gaze at his face. Not unusual for any infant, Christian spent long periods of time fascinated at seeing his reflection. He was often nose-to-nose with the delightful face looking back at him. Standing at his bedroom doorway, peering in, but frozen in place, repetitive, gnawing, anxiety-invoking questions came to my mind: Will he come to know he has a disability? Will he be aware that he is mentally challenged? Will he be cognizant that he will need open heart surgery and feel the stress and agony of that procedure? Will Christian identify that his features resemble a subset of our population with the label of *Down syndrome*? When should I tell him about his diagnosis? Should I tell him at all?

Growing older, Christian's fascination with looking in the mirror has not waned. As a toddler, riding in his stroller in the clothing stores, Christian would crane his neck sideways to hold the last glimpse of himself as I hurried along to the next clothing rack. As he got a little older, attempts to leave the stroller or pull away from holding my hand were often made so that he could go find a mirror. It was difficult to leave a dressing room that had a mirror in it or a store with wonderfully large mirrors because

Christian was hopping from foot to foot, wagging an invisible tail, or presenting a non-verbal monologue to his captivated, one-child audience. In our bathroom, a 20x magnification mirror sits on the vanity. I am often invited to the mirror play by Christian, crooking his arm around my neck pulling me into view of the glass porthole. I resist looking into a device that magnifies my facial flaws, but Christian delights in all his facial features and expressions. Christian and I are cheek-to-cheek, staring into the mirror. We are looking at the same two faces, the same images in the mirror but with individual perspectives.

Many of us see people and immediately judge them on their outward appearance, categorizing them by race, culture, body shape, facial appearance, and so on. Over the past century, labels for a person such as Christian have evolved from terms such as *retarded* and *disabled* to *special needs*. The most acceptable label currently is *person with special needs*, putting the person before the label. If you really think about it, we all have special needs—needs to avoid things that make us anxious and to seek things that calm us, needs to nurture our souls, needs to avoid situations that trigger anger, and needs to find ways to resolve problems.

Questions as to whether or not to tell Christian about his diagnosis began to melt away as I observed him looking at his own reflection. Christian is likely not thinking *Should I label characteristics about you, Mom? Should I describe your myriad personality deficits or physical flaws?* I think Christian may be saying *I like what I see. I don't need to know what anyone thinks of me or what group or category anyone puts me in.*

Christian is enough for himself. He has no need for labels or for another's approval. The social labels such as *disabled*, *retarded*, *intellectually-impaired*, and *developmentally delayed* have no relevance to Christian. He's concerned only that he is well-cared for and loved.

Christian's concept of the future is likely limited to the immediate situation, perhaps out to the next few days but probably not beyond that time frame. There may be a peacefulness of heart in Christian, without the anxiety of future or worldly complications that many of us carry. Christian has given me the strength to see him and see myself as God sees us, without labeling, categorizing, or judging, and with pure, unconditional love reflected in our image in the mirror.

Beloved, I pray that all may go well with you and that you may be in good health, just as it is well with your soul.

—1 John 1:2

L E S S O N 9

FOOD

When Christian was born, he was not strong enough to drink from a bottle or breastfeed due to his heart defect and overall muscle weakness. I worried so much. I believed he might never eat regular food. Tube feeding via his nose was the only way he could receive nutrition, in addition to occasional (yet ineffective) sucking on bottles of defrosted breast milk. No cradling him in my arms as he nursed or took a bottle. No watching his fluttering eyelids drop him gently into a peaceful sleep. How different it was from what I expected, and I was saddened by the loss in remembering this time with my first-born. A wonderful, caring nurse came to our house several times per week those first three months to help Christian get stronger and healthier so that he could undergo heart surgery; ten pounds was the goal. Heavens! His uncle weighed that at birth, and Christian was approaching three months of age.

With no medical background and a general aversion to anything medical in general, I watched my husband, Dave, as he lovingly inserted the surprisingly long feeding tube into Christian's nose. I then checked that it properly settled into his stomach, as instructed by the nurse. However, Christian developed a regular knack for tucking his pinky finger under the only tubing not taped to his face and flinging it out of his nose. Together, Dave and I worked at occupying Christian's busy little hands as we reinserted the tube, and we became quite expert in the procedure quickly.

Christian reached his target weight and did very well in heart surgery. The second day after surgery, he drank more from a bottle than at any time during those first three months, and we rejoiced. Looking back, I gained an appreciation for my husband that I may not have experienced otherwise, and I recall Dave stating matter-of-factly, "You do what you have to do."

The special lesson that Christian unknowingly taught Dave and me about how to work together for the good of the team was invaluable. Dave and I came up with clever ways to integrate healthy foods into Christian's diet, given that his personal choice menu in his early years consisted of only about eight items. I honed what little cooking and meal preparation creativity skills I possessed by masquerading vegetables in fruit smoothies, with strainer at the ready. Sometimes it took participation by the other team members—his siblings Matt and Amanda—to show Christian how really wonderful broccoli could be. They were often Christian's cheerleaders, and now all three of our kids sit at the table and share a pizza.

Christian eventually worked through most of his aversions and now eats more foods than I can count. An inspiration to us, he isn't interested in the vast array of cookies and candies and has no cavities to date. Christian loves all things food: meal time, snacks, bed-time treats of applesauce, crackers, or yogurt, eating out, eating in, picnics, and eating in the car on a long trip. Although the journey wasn't always satisfying, we now delight in Christian's appreciation of food.

There is nothing better for mortals than to eat and drink, and find enjoyment in their toil.

—Ecclesiastes 2:24

LESSON 10

DONUTS

Everyone has a favorite food. Christian's is donuts—plain, old-fashioned ones. Donuts are his particular treat. Birthdays are full of contentment for Christian when he is given a plate of donuts with a candle in one. No need for expensive, themed cakes—just donuts. Every year we ask, "What do you want to eat for your birthday?" Christian's reply is always the same, "Donuts." But we ask anyway.

We learned to cover the other donuts on the plate just before he blows out the candle, as his stream of air often has an accompaniment of saliva. The candle is placed just out of reach because the first time Christian noticed a candle on his donut he promptly extinguished the flame between his thumb and forefinger. The perplexed look on his face soon vanished with the first delectable bite of his birthday treat.

When Christian eats a donut, there is a three-foot radius of donut crumbs on the kitchen floor and a remarkable number of crumbs down his shirt (despite the bib), and in his diaper. How does that happen? I have always been a neat freak, and I feel my anxiety rise as donut crumbs replicate exponentially. "Relax, Mom. The dog will get the crumbs," my children exclaim. I have never seen a person eat a food item and smile at the same time, savoring every delicious bite. But Christian does, twisting and turning the round delicacy until he finds just the right spot to sink his teeth into. Instead of running for the hand vacuum, I remind myself to sit back and just watch what God truly intended for us regarding eating—take time to savor and enjoy the goodness of food. I admit I have served his treat outside on the deck, but mostly, I try to let my fastidiousness and neatness crumble like donuts.

Let the little children come to me, and do not stop them; for it is to such as these that the kingdom of heaven belongs.

—Matthew 19:14

PLAY

Early on, I assumed I would never have leisure time for myself, nor could I relax as a parent of a child with special needs. My thoughts were so negative: *He'll probably need someone to sit and play with him all day. I have another child who needs some of my attention. I won't have the time or the energy to attend to him all day.*

Fast forward to Christian at age eleven, as I listen from the kitchen down into the basement and hear *crack, crack, crack.* And I am calm because it is the wonderful sound of pool balls expertly striking each other for that perfect shot. Christian uses his hands and has invented a game of solitaire on the pool table in which pool sticks are not needed. Ahh, another skilled throw of the eight ball banked off the side wall into the corner pocket; the professionals would marvel! Satisfaction gleams on Christian's face as the last ball lands squarely in the far right corner, keen eye and skilled moves at the ready when he takes all the balls out to start over again.

Christian defines leisure and play time differently than most of us do. There is joy in the moment of playing, in the activity itself—not necessarily in the outcome.

We have an air hockey table in the basement. Friends and family instruct Christian in the rules, "Christian, keep it out! Keep the puck out! Block your goal."

Christian lovingly guides our puck into his goal, with a beaming smile, implying, *I did it! Another one for me! You lose!*

Lose yourself in the fun of the moment; it's a lesson for everyone to learn.

Computer and video games are not on my list of special talents. If there is a wall to run into or a cliff to go over with my computer character, I find the obstacle very quickly, and the game is over. Christian discovered my husband's iPhone with the *Temple Run* game on it and was intrigued. I immediately thought *There is no way Christian will understand how to run, jump, turn, slide and tilt to get the character through the maze.* Wrong again! My high score pales in comparison to Christian's score. He can maneuver this game from set up to completion without any help from me at all. He has discovered many games and stories on the iPad and spends quiet time in his room, where I go up to check on him because he is quiet and happy at play.

For where your treasure is, there your heart will be also.

—Matthew 6:21

LESSON 12

BED TIME

Bed time can be challenging for any parent, especially the parent of little children or teens. Early on, I thought it would be difficult to have a child with limited understanding grasp the importance of a good night's sleep. However, most evenings, when Christian hears the word *bed*, he heads right for the stairs to his room. Once, we inadvertently said the word *bed* in a conversation before it was actually Christian's bed time, only to find him kneeling next to the bed with his body bent over and the top half of him on the bed, sound asleep. He must have gotten tired of waiting for us to tuck him in, so he put himself to bed.

Before Christian could walk, I sewed all the legs of his pajamas together to keep his legs from flopping over to either side as he slept. I had read in a medical textbook that this might reduce hip problems later in life. Once Christian could get out of bed alone, I had to abandon the mummy pants so he wouldn't trip, and instead, use pillows to therapeutically prop his knees together. Each morning I would find all his therapeutic pillows discarded and scattered about on the floor. Christian's special pillow, however, remained tucked safely and securely under his head, just where he wanted it, sending the message, *Let's not think about later, Mom; I want every night right now to be special.*

Christian can't perform the nighttime routine to get ready for bed by himself, even at age thirteen, but he can do most of the preparation activities with a little help, such as brushing his teeth and changing into his pajamas. Although there are busy nights when Dave and I want to shoo him off on his own, we are reminded that our other two kids no longer seek us out to tuck them into bed, so we get to enjoy this quiet togetherness each night with Christian.

Christian says a close rendition of a prayer that Dave made up for him when he was a baby, and Christian will assist you in properly positioning your hands in prayer if you forget. The prayer goes like this:

Thank you, Father, for giving us this day.
Thank you for letting us work and play.
Please bless everyone that we love,
Here on earth and up above.

At bed time, a favorite pillow is a must for lots of people, including Christian. "Grandma, he needs another one," my call to Grandma beckons. Grandma Gloria is happy to know that her skills are especially appreciated by Christian, as she made the very first pillow he fell in love with. When a grin reaches the pillow that is nestling Christian's head, we know he has found true happiness. Every night, Christian places his special pillow in the perfect position. Then the covers come up all the way under his chin, and his arms get tucked under so only the knuckles and fingertips stick out. A hug and a kiss on the cheek, followed by a flip of the night light, conclude the evening procedure, and we are out the door. Thirteen years have passed, and Christian still enjoys his special routine, special room, special pillow, and special hugs. He might resist in the future, but for now, I am enjoying Christian's delight in this ritual at bed time.

Little children, let us love, not in word or speech, but in truth and action.

—1 John 3:18

WORDS

Christian has a lot to communicate; however, he doesn't have a lot to say in words. As an infant, we began signing, and Christian learned some important signs such as *eat* and *more*. Really, what else is there at that age? As Christian got older, we weren't sure what would be the best way for him to communicate—signing, speaking, pictures, or computers, so we tried them all. Each of us has a unique preference and aptitude for certain tasks. For Christian, communication is primarily with words and gestures and sometimes pictures to help schedule and organize tasks. For the most part, we understand him. Sometimes we do not. It is remarkable how adept we have become at figuring out what Christian wants. This is a skill our whole family is quite proud of, as we exclaim to a new friend, "Oh, Christian wants to do X, Y, or Z when he does that motion."

Christian often prefers to take me by the hand and guide me to what he wants, as I gently coax and cue him, saying, "Use your words, Christian." Skillful at getting what he wants (and very clever, I might add), Christian has devised numerous mannerisms and gestures, despite his difficulty in getting the words out. Sitting patiently in front of the closed pantry door with his legs crossed lets us know that his favorite cereal lies just beyond reach. Bringing a movie to me with arms rigid and forward, head tilted sideways and eyes uplifted for his cutest coaxing clearly implies *Mom, would you play this for me?* Words are not needed when we come across Christian sitting in his specially modified chair (Dave fastened a platform to the chair's legs so Christian's feet don't dangle) in the breakfast room because he would like a snack, if you please.

Christian makes himself quite clear with an outstretched arm, index finger pointed down with emphasis to the cup of juice that sits obviously in front of us but that we neglected to place near enough for him to reach. Or, Christian will point to the basketballs on the shelf in the garage by repeatedly bending and straightening his right arm because he is pretty sure he has time for a few shots before the bus comes. The speech-language pathologist hat that I have donned for twenty-eight years comes out as I request encouragingly, "Say it louder, Christian. Slow down. Use your light voice. Yes we know what you want, but say it with words."

I imagine Christian's thoughts are, *But you know what I want. I showed you and you love me and know me, so we're good, right?* I mostly wear the mommy hat and not the speech therapist hat.

Christian loves to watch his favorite story series, *Peep and the Big Wide World* on the iPad. To our dismay, he regularly switches the controls from English to Spanish. None of us in the house speaks Spanish, beyond a few, groping, over-learned utterances from high school or college. Christian immerses himself in the story and watches the actions, apparently fully grasping the antics of his favorite bird characters, despite not understanding one word they are saying (or so we think). Perhaps he knows more Spanish than we all do. Communication trumps words.

How very good and pleasant it is when kindred live together in unity!

—Psalm 133:1

L E S S O N 1 4

SMILES

I remember when Christian's smiles were not a source of joy because, as his teeth grew, two of them became as sharp as daggers. Weak mouth muscles cause his lips to be apart and his tongue to protrude, which is a problem during a fall if you have slow reflexes and do not block the fall with your hands. On two occasions before the age of five (sparing the gory details), Christian fell on the pavement and landed on his face, causing severe injuries to his tongue. How do you prevent falls? He's a kid; he's going to fall down. So we reversed our thinking. If we can't keep him from falling, maybe we can help ease the damage to the tongue. A wonderful dentist rounded the teeth with an instrument so that they would not puncture his tongue. Voilà!

Christian's early dental problem was a source of heartache for us and very painful for him. Those memories are erased more and more each time Christian smiles. The most amazing thing about Christian smiling is not just the feeling you get when he smiles at you but the personal smile he experiences on his own time when no one is around. I find this fascinating. I peek in on Christian frequently during the day while he is playing, and very often I find him smiling at nothing in particular. He is not just sitting with a pleasant or neutral look on his face, he is smiling. Displaying a great big, tooth-bearing, eyes closed, head tilted back smile, as if Rodney Dangerfield just provided his best one liner. Christian doesn't verbalize what, at that moment, causes him such joy, and he shouldn't have to tell me.

Psychologists say if you smile, even if it is a mechanical, prompted smile, that the feel-good hormones in your body increase and you become happier for the moment. We should all do what Christian does on a regular basis to feel good, and that is smile.

Love one another with mutual affection; outdo one another in showing honor.

—Romans 12:10

L E S S O N   1 5

HUGS

Although my two other children argue that it is not cool to give hugs to Mom or Dad, we can always count on Christian to come to the rescue. Oh, I occasionally get a superficial, pacifying hug from Matt or Amanda. You know the kind, where their body stiffens and they remain just long enough to be polite and move on quickly to something else. A hug from Christian is as if time has stopped and neither of us cares one bit if the world ends at that very moment. Christian's hugs are the kind of hugs that melt your soul, like hot chocolate sauce does over vanilla ice cream. You have to get one of these hugs from Christian to know what I am talking about.

Christian gives hugs freely to anyone and at any time. Christian does not possess the social skills to understand when a hug would be considered appropriate, and, as parents, we conscientiously try to teach Christian allowable situations for hugging. Reminders include giving a same-aged peer a high-five and not hugging a stranger, but Christian prefers to hug anyway. Perhaps the world would be a better place all around if more of us hugged more often.

Sometimes, according to Christian, I don't give the hug correctly. If I forget to wrap my arms around his back, he lifts them up for me and places them in the correct spot. *Do not skimp on my hug, Mom*, he may be thinking. A trying day seems less so after a hug from Christian, with his head nuzzling your neck like a newborn cub snuggling the soft fur of the mother bear. Seldom is there a time I am not glad I interrupted the hectic commotion to share a hug.

I will give thanks to the Lord because of His righteousness and will sing praise to the name of the Lord, the Most High.

—Psalm 7:17

LESSON 16

GOD

I reluctantly admit I questioned God's intention, and yes, there was a period of anger toward God after Christian was born. After all, I worked with special needs children in my occupation as a speech-language pathologist. I volunteered to be a hugger at the Knights of Columbus' Special Olympics. I regularly tossed my change in the collection bucket at stop lights to help the developmentally delayed. Why had God missed all this? Why was he giving me this burden? I think God heard all my thoughts and simply smiled down on me expressing *Just wait.*

Our family says a prayer at dinner every night. Many nights, the four of us (Christian excluded) make the sign of the cross lackadaisically, probably thinking of what fun activity we'll get to do right after dinner. Some nights, we all just watch Christian make the sign of the cross, indicating Father, Son, Holy Spirit. Christian's eyes are sometimes closed, and he touches each location—forehead, chest, shoulder, shoulder—deliberately and with precision. He's reminding us, imploring us to truly know, feel, and thank God for our blessings.

On a typical Sunday morning at church when Christian was about ten, the priest's homily explained the importance of professing faith and living as a good model to others by stating, "All Christians, stand up for your beliefs." To our surprise, Christian stood up promptly on the pew. Tall! Proud! Of course he did not realize the actual meaning of what the priest was saying, but there he stood as a model for those around him, accompanied by a few stifled giggles by church attendees. I think God has a sense of humor. I think God regularly delights in his beautiful creation that is Christian.

In our faith as Christians, we believe that heaven and eternal glory with the heavenly Father after death is a gift received by accepting Jesus as savior while here on earth. Each person after the age of reason, according to the Bible, decides for himself or herself to accept or deny Jesus. Children with intellectual impairments receive a *get-in-free* pass to heaven because of their limited comprehension. Dave and I have tremendous peace in knowing that we will be forever united with Christian in heaven.

I questioned God's plan for Christian in our lives when he was a baby, and I asked God, "*Why* me?" Knowing Christian now as I do, when Christian and I get to heaven, I plan to walk up to my heavenly Father, hand-in-hand with my son, not in self-pity but in tremendous gratitude that I have been allowed to look directly and daily into His eyes through Christian and ask, "Why *me?*" Now I know to trust God.

Love is patient; love is kind; love is not envious or boastful or arrogant or rude. It does not insist on its own way; it is not irritable or resentful; it does not rejoice in wrongdoing, but rejoices in the truth. It bears all things, believes all things, hopes all things, endures all things.

—1 Corinthians 12:4–7

L E S S O N   1 7

DAD

Everyone should have a best friend. For Christian, it's his dad, Dave. I'm a close second, tied with his brother and sister. There is no sadness for me as Christian often bypasses me to get to his dad, and I grin from deep within my heart for the special bond between Dave and Christian. Maybe it's the tickle game before bed as I enter Christian's room, hearing a semblance of "Mommy, go way." Maybe it's that Christian knew from the very first moment of his life that his Dad accepted him unconditionally, without question or concern. Maybe it's the basketball games. Maybe it's that Christian sensed Dave's insight over the first few months of Christian's life: "You aren't feeling sorry for Christian and what he might feel about his life in the future, Kathy, but rather, you are feeling sorry for yourself about what you believe Christian's future will be like. Just look at him, Kathy. Does he appear sad and worried to you?"

At that moment, I recall a happy infant trying desperately to reach his elusive toes, all the while enjoying the chase with a smile and a giggle. I waited for Dave to feel the way I did when we first learned the news about Christian—disappointed, angry, resentful, but he never did. I don't know why Dave never felt the feelings that I felt. Right after Christian was born, Dave unwaveringly informed our parents that, indeed, Christian had

Down syndrome, but in his exact words, "He's just another little boy, only a little different."

Dave repeatedly reminded me in my moments of pity over Christian's limitations, "I just want to enjoy our son." Wise words and a fearless resolve echoed daily from Dave's lips and from his spirit in those early years.

As Christian got older, Dave sought out many opportunities to enjoy his son. After work, Dave would take the steps upstairs by twos to change his clothes so he could shoot a few hoops with Christian before dinner. "Swish. Money in the bank. Chuck it from the cheap seats, Christian," I would hear Dave say from the driveway out front.

I have no idea how a child whom I recall could barely hold a rattle when he was four months old could put a regulation sized ball into a hoop at regulation height when he was only three-and-a-half feet tall! I would call out several times for the *boys* to come in to eat dinner, only to hear Dave respond, "Just a few more minutes, please."

Over the years, Christian and his dad have shared many special moments. Whether those moments involved whopping excitement in bouncing wildly while tubing on the lake or quiet solitude while rocking on a porch swing contentment always emanates around them as they play or sit together.

Companionship during the mundane tasks in life is elevated because of the bond Christian and Dave have developed. Walking the dog, caring for the lawn, and grilling hotdogs are so enjoyable for Christian and his dad because they are doing these tasks together. Sometimes Christian and Dave say absolutely nothing to each other but simply share an occasional glance; the bond is extraordinary between Christian and his Dad.

I have indeed received much joy and encouragement from your love, because the hearts of the saints have been refreshed through you, my brother.

—Philemon 4:7

L E S S O N   1 8

BROTHER

I recall a time when Christian was three months old and his brother, Matt, was three-and-a-half years old. Matt was stroking Christian's cheek with his pinky finger as Christian lay recovering in the intensive care unit after his first heart surgery.

"Don't disturb him. He needs rest. Be careful of the tube in his nose," I said to Matt. "I will," Matt replied.

I also recall Matt at ten years of age, again stroking Christian's cheek with his pinky finger in recovery after his second heart surgery.

"I know Mom. Be careful of the tubes. Let him rest."

I assumed there would be resentment of Christian from Matt, as my attention shifted to the child who needed it most. Our home seemed to have a revolving door with all the therapists coming and going for the first three years of early intervention services. During that time, my attention was regularly divided when I was observing the therapists teaching Christian basic skills, while pretending at the same time to be Buzz Lightyear with Matt. There were many trips to the doctors' offices, where Matt had to learn to entertain himself. Not a bad skill for a first-born to learn, I might add.

In the early years with Christian, a *divide and conquer* mentality was rampant in our family because Christian needed special attention on vacations near oceans, in busy amusement parks, and on campgrounds. We did our best to find cohesion, but I sometimes felt guilty when I had to split off separately with Christian because it was unsafe for him to participate in a certain activity. I waited for the resentment to come, to see Matt lash out in some way at Christian, but it never happened. I think Matt learned compassion instead. I'm not sure he would have learned such compassion if we didn't have Christian.

Years later, I see our rough and tough teenager, Matt, trying to catch a hug or a snuggle from Christian before one of them leaves for school. Matt seeks Christian out first when he returns from overnight sports camps, bypassing me as if I were invisible. I often find Matt in Christian's room after he has drifted off to sleep, kneeling by his bed, staring at him, or stroking his forehead or cheek. I think Matt is praying, although I don't pry. I wonder if Matt is thanking God for allowing his awesome little brother to be just the way he is or if he's asking God for guidance about how best to take care of someone so very special—a job fitting for a faithful big brother.

She opens her mouth with wisdom and the teaching of kindness is on her tongue.

—Proverbs 31:26–27

LESSON 19

SISTER

Dave and I had our date night timed so perfectly.

"Christian had a poop earlier today. Let's go out on the town alone. His sister can play with him, and Matt is old enough to babysit Christian," said Dave.

Not long into our amazing dinner, complete with white linen tablecloths and a generous pour of the house cabernet, Dave's cell phone rang with a slightly frantic sixteen-year-old calling a code brown (also known as *poopy diaper*).

"I got this Mom," shouts Amanda in the background over Matt's cell phone. "You guys stay out and have fun," I hear her say over the roar of the ventilator fan in the powder room bathroom. Our ten-year-old daughter is once again stepping up to the plate to take care of business.

Last-born children can be notorious for being dependent and babied, compared to the first born, with typical bragging rights of independence and self-sufficiency, according to the psychological literature. Our daughter apparently didn't read the psychology books because she was wiping food off of Christian's chin in their side-by-side high chairs before she could walk. She would position his legs, using the proper technique for crawling and standing, and remove any items she deemed *danerus* (i.e., dangerous) from within three feet of his grasp before she turned four.

Because Christian and Amanda were born only fourteen months apart, I heard many people say (out of ear shot, they thought), when I was pregnant with Amanda, "She's crazy for having another baby so close to Christian, you know, with all his issues." Three kids under age five can be harrowing for any parent. I would take all three kids to the shallow end of the neighborhood pool. I'd put Amanda in a bathtub ring, with one of my feet securing it, hold Christian on my lap because he couldn't sit fully upright, and swear an eternal time-out for Matt if he got anywhere even close to the deep end.

Christian and Amanda started walking around the same time because of his delay and her precociousness. Yes, it was overwhelming and crazy. Isn't it for all moms with little ones? It wasn't as much Christian's disability as it was that both he and Amanda were young and into everything all at once. In addition, I had a third, very active child in the mix.

One proud mommy moment involving Amanda took place at one of our favorite campsites when she was about 10 years old. Twin boys with autism were being verbally harassed by a group of young teenagers at the playground. Before I could step in, I witnessed Amanda calling the teens over to her.

"Excuse me. Can I talk to you? Those boys have something called autism. So they aren't trying to act inappropriately or silly and aren't trying to be mean. Try to understand how hard it is for them to play the way we can and try to be a friend."

I almost fell over. Those were Amanda's exact words. The teen girls shrugged and walked away but did not harass the boys the rest of that day. Amanda gravitates toward any person, especially a child, in need of help. She always has a kind or encouraging word to say or a gentle way of resting her hand on a needy person's shoulder for comfort. Dave and I don't doubt that whatever career Amanda chooses will be one that allows her to share her gifts of kindness and empathy.

I don't regret that Amanda was born so close in age to Christian. Although I worried about Christian, as Amanda rapidly surpassed him in all the milestones, I now smile looking back at how she became a protective, dependable, loving caregiver at a very young age. With a devoted heart and for whom no request is too big, one of the best gifts ever given to Christian was his little sister.

God made everything that creeps upon the ground of every kind. And God saw that it was good.

—Genesis 1:25

LESSON 20

STUEY

Stuey is our dog. I didn't like dogs most of my life. I'm not a dog person, as they say. After three years of Matt and Amanda begging for a dog, and hearing that animals can be good for children with special needs, I grudgingly gave in.

Stuey came from the shelter as a puppy; he was part beagle and part something unknown but likely very large. I held my breath as we began to integrate Stuey into our home—fully anticipating repeated headaches I believed would come with having a pet that's not in a fish bowl or an aquarium.

The bond between Christian and Stuey is beyond anything I might have expected. Mostly I believed indifference or tolerance would prevail, one toward the other. "Don't stand on the dog, Christian," I say. Stuey's head tilts up toward Christian as if to say, *Yeah, don't stand on me, but I don't mind, 'cause you're not very big.* It's a small price for Stuey to pay given countless hours he and Christian spend lying nose to nose, just staring, understanding the needs of each other.

As is typical, Matt and Amanda mostly go about their daily business without including Stuey; morning routines include shooing Stuey out of the way as he wags his tail, furiously seeking a pat on the head. Promises made for daily walking Stuey around the block are broken. The task of feeding Stuey has, as expected, been handed over to me. The amusement of seeing Stuey's body shake with delight when he hears the can of food hit the counter has worn off for Matt and Amanda. For Christian, however, there is new joy in all these chores each day.

Christian's morning routine is not complete without a visit with Stuey. Whether it's giving Stuey a full-body hug (including arms and legs), lying next to Stuey on the foam bed in the hallway, stroking Stuey's floppy ears, or pulling Stuey through the dining room with the stuffing-less animal toy hanging from his mouth, Christian happily starts his day. Walking Stuey is joyful for Christian, as shown by the way he skips alongside of Stuey, head tilting side to side. Christian appears pleased and proud when we give him Stuey's leash to hold, although we are careful to unobtrusively hold on to a part of the leash because Christian sometimes lets go without warning.

Meal times for Stuey are better if Christian is around, but we provide frequent reminders to him so that he doesn't offer Stuey table food, especially his very delicious and juicy grapes (harmful to dogs if swallowed). Reminders given to Christian also include not allowing Stuey to lick his entire face after eating salty potato chips or nibble on his fingers to receive morsels of left-over hotdog scraps.

I haven't entirely changed. I'm still not a dog person. However, I regularly witness Christian cuddling with Stuey and stroking the dog's ears with the tenderness we've shown to Christian over the years, and it melts me. I find it heart-warming that Christian and Stuey fully and completely love each other. Christian has taught me that it may be possible one day for me to love our dog Stuey.

Faithful friends are a sturdy shelter: whoever finds one has found a treasure.

—Sirach 6:14

LESSON 21

FRIENDS

Dave and I wondered if Christian would be capable of having friends. Despite efforts in our country over the last few decades to increase awareness about children with special needs, I still witness children who stare at Christian and then turn and run from him as he approaches to play with them. As a mother, this is heart-breaking. The good thing is that Christian is relatively unaware of this reaction to him and usually will just go in another direction to seek out a willing playmate. Sometimes I intervene and explain something to the effect that children with Down syndrome look a little different and may not talk very much, but they love to have fun and play, whatever game is being played. Then I wait, hoping that one of the children will reach out to Christian or say, "Come on, we're playing tag" or "We're going to climb on the monkey bars; wanna come?" Sometimes they include him, but mostly they don't.

For Christian, if children are playing, he is ready to join the fun, whether he knows them or not; there are no barriers as to how a person looks, speaks, or acts. Christian is an immediate friend. He will not judge you, bully you, or glance sideways at you while whispering to another person. Never did. Never will. Christian is immune to stares, harsh words, and heads turning away from him. He will clap when you make a good shot and say,

"Your turn," even when it is not really your turn. He will smile at you and generally make your game better. Sometimes he just likes to sit and watch other children play, as if to say, *Have fun out there, okay?* We should all learn from Christian about how to be accepting friends.

Speak evil of no one, avoid quarreling, be gentle
and show every courtesy to everyone.

—Titus 3:2

L E S S O N   2 2

NEIGHBORS

Good neighbors help each other, share fun times together or, at least, exchange friendly waves over the hedges. During Christian's early years, I resigned myself to isolation so as to appear strong and resilient. I avoided many social settings to avoid embarrassment and I conjured ridicule I believed would inevitably occur should Christian have a meltdown. I assumed Christian's gestures, vocal outbursts, and behaviors would scare people off. With a few exceptions, this proved not to be the case.

A few days after Christian's second heart surgery, the doorbell rang. As I answered the door, I found a smiling neighbor whose daughter I knew through our church. We exchanged niceties then she declared, "I heard you are heading back to the hospital to stay with Christian so we are not asking *if* we can watch your other children but *when* you would like us to come." I stood in the doorway and cried because I had not heard an offer for babysitting presented in such an affirmative manner and I was overwhelmed with appreciation. There were few groceries in the house, due to our round-the-clock shifts with Christian in the ICU and Dave needed to return to work, so I accepted their offer and was glad that I abandoned my stubbornness.

My negative thinking in Christian's early years told me that his unpredictable conduct and limited communication skills would keep anyone I asked from agreeing to watch him while I ran errands. In lieu of asking someone to babysit, I either didn't get things done or I over-burdened myself when Dave was home. Over time, I discovered that Christian had become a special needs student teacher magnet in our neighborhood, and we were flooded with calls from young adults majoring in special education. Occasionally, a babysitter would come to the door with a lesson plan, and it was really endearing to watch him/her *establish rapport with the child*, and *offer two simple options for the child to nonverbally select*, listed items one and two on the lesson plan. For these young adults, babysitting Christian was their first mini classroom, and Christian had some teaching to do! Offering training in patience and opportunities to decipher what Christian was trying to communicate added new lessons to these future teachers.

Surprising to me one day, over our backyard fence, I heard someone say, "Can I come over and watch Christian play? I've never seen a kid have more fun on a Slip-N-Slide. It's pretty entertaining." I have received pleasant comments such as, "It's really cute when Christian plays volleyball in the pool" or "Christian looks so serious bringing the recycling cans to the curb; it's as if he were in the Strongest Man Competition." It is a rare occurrence that Christian and I are subjected to ridicule and scorn as I thought might occur.

I still haven't figured out how to be in two places at once and I have improved in my ability to ask a neighbor to come to the rescue. In many cultures, neighbors hold the same value as family members because they are immediately available to meet one another's needs. Some of us who have children with special needs gravitate toward one another, creating a micro-community to share the challenges faced and reciprocate support. There is comfort in knowing that others share your daily challenges, obvious when you exchange that *I get it* look. It takes courage to integrate your child with special needs into the community. It takes humility to admit that you need help. Go fearlessly out into your neighborhood with your child—you may find that people are accommodating and friendly if given the chance.

A kind word, a look of understanding, or an offer to lend a helping hand can be a precious gift from a caring neighbor.

We have gifts that differ according to the grace given to us.

—Romans 12:6

LESSON 23

TEACHERS

Our school district has provided many excellent teachers for our other children, Matt and Amanda, over the years—and then there are Christian's teachers. The compassion and competency of Christian's special education teachers are beyond measure. I never expected their unsolicited calls just to share their joy when Christian accomplished a drum rhythm exceeding the visiting doctoral student's expectations. Nor did I anticipate the warm smiles and words of appreciation Christian received as he delivered refreshments to the staff on *Coffee Shop Friday*. Frequent, heart-warming reports described how so many of the regular education children and staff call Christian by name in the halls and give him a high-five as he completes his assignment of taking the attendance forms to the office.

Countless hours, beyond school time, were spent by many of Christian's teachers to compose hand-written notes about novel ideas for reinforcing good behavior. Phone calls were made by the educational team to provide a detailed description of a new program to help improve Christian's reading skills or to offer suggestions to compensate for his vision deficits—just a few examples emphasizing their dedication to Christian.

When I attend Christian's annual IEP meetings (short for Individualized Education Plan), the team places a box of tissues within my reach. I have not been to an IEP meeting yet when I did not shed tears of true gratitude to the teachers, nurses, therapists, and administrators who work with Christian. Sometimes I catch a tear or two welling up in their eyes as well.

Year after year, I am astounded by the detailed observations and description of all of Christian's nuances with regard to his learning style, behavioral needs, strengths, and areas of challenge, as well as their suggestions for maximizing his abilities in both the life skills and educational arenas. We are fortunate to have found some of the world's best teachers.

Let them praise his name with dancing, making melody to him with tambourine and lyre. For the Lord takes pleasure in his people.

—Psalm 149:3–4

DANCE

When the music plays, you dance, no matter where, no matter when, no matter who is watching. That's Christian's attitude toward dance: utter freedom and happiness for how the music makes him feel and what he wants to experience through the music at that moment. From the time he could sit up, Christian danced, even if just by squatting rhythmically to the beat or pumping his arms up and down in his car seat. We recently heard from his teachers that Christian is quite good on the bongo drums, with rhythm, timing, and enthusiasm accompanied by head bobs and weaves.

Christian regularly provides us with belly laughs in the way he moves with a sideways leg swing none of us can duplicate. Sometimes we dance with Christian and sometimes we sit back and watch his whole being exude joy, energy, and abandon in every movement for as long as the music plays. Frequently we catch Christian dancing when no one is around, and no audible sound can be heard. Perhaps he's creating a symphony or concert in his mind for his pleasure, alone, as he sways and spins with a contented smile on his face.

I should not be surprised about Christian's natural inclination toward dance, given the fact that I have been dancing since age six and still take dance classes at fifty-something. Dance has reminded me that Christian is not just a child with Down syndrome and the stuff that goes with his *disorder* but that he is a Murray, with all his Murray family's traits, abilities, weaknesses, and flaws.

Early in Christian's life, I put him in the Down syndrome box before I put him in the Murray box, missing the intricacies of his genetic structure that he shares with each and every family member. I narrowed his opportunities for artistic expression, given my expectations for skills that a person with Down syndrome would likely have.

I have come to realize that a diagnosis does not define how your life will play out. Labels and descriptions do not dictate what will please the heart or fill the soul. Christian is completely unaware of what the experts or the books say he likely will or will not do. He simply wants the freedom to do what makes him happy, including the freedom to dance.

For you shall go out in joy, and be led back in peace; the mountains and the hills before you shall burst into song, and all the trees of the field shall clap their hands.

—Isaiah 55:12

LESSON 25

WAITING

Most people hate waiting, except Christian. He can turn waiting into playing with ease. Year round, our driveway is also Christian's bus stop for school. Because there are children on Christian's bus with various physical and behavioral needs, wait times can vary considerably. In the spring time, our driveway becomes Christian's wonderland of *twirly-birds* (i.e., seeds) from our huge maple tree. I see the newly-fallen seeds as future hours of sweeping or weeding before the seeds take root in the garden or in the sidewalk cracks. Christian sees these seeds as scattered toys for his personal delight as he grabs handfuls, tosses them in the air, and enjoys the fanciful flight each one makes to a place of rest. There's no concern for time, and there's full immersion in the beauty of the activity.

Summer time offers endless possibilities for shadow art at the driveway bus stop, with Christian bending, jumping, and balancing to create unique, one-dimensional black sculptures. After intensely staring and marveling at his creations, Christian pulls me into the game to form shapes of my own rather than check messages on my phone, gather the mail from the mailbox (forgotten from the previous day), or collect stray litter that has drifted into our yard. I realize that I rather enjoy the whimsy and childhood delight in this game.

Fall miraculously transforms standing and waiting for the bus into genuine appreciation for nature's splendor as Christian closely examines then twists and flips multicolored leaves between his fingers. I foresee heating pads on sore muscles following hours of raking and bagging leaves or scraping leaves from the mulch. When I allow myself time to sit with Christian on the bench in front of the house, I realize he's sitting with such stillness, as if God is whispering in his ear at that very moment. Christian's eyes gaze at the prairie grass taking a few final bows before exiting for the season. Never before have I looked at prairie grass intently to realize the grace and delicacy of the dancing stems.

Winter time waiting for the bus offers snowy footprint trails stomped out into swirling circles, which find their way in no particular direction. Never mind that all of that snow will need to be cleared. If we are lucky enough and the snow is falling, Christian tilts his head back in wonderment, perhaps thinking carefully as to how one small snowflake can sting for a split second, tickle as it drips down his warm cheek, then disappear. Christian does not tell me what to do but physically positions me directly behind him in our own personal conga line to make matching footprints in the fallen snow. Glancing over his shoulder now and then to be sure I have not stepped out of line, we prance all over the driveway until there are no remaining clear paths to take. My clear path is to allow Christian to guide me in appreciation of the moment. Giving myself permission, I am distracted, learning how to be happy and still while waiting.

I will make all my goodness pass before you.

—Exodus 33:19

RIDES

"Want to go for a ride, Christian? Up and at 'em then," Dave says bright and early to Christian, who usually wakes just as the crickets are getting to sleep. No delay. No protest. No complaint. The vehicle does not matter: car, bus, boat, wagon, tube, sled. Christian is up for anything that he can ride in. Offers for early morning rides to the local Dunkin Donuts, afternoon rides to the park, or evening rides around the block are all received with an affirmative, exaggerated head nod of yes from Christian. Sitting cross-legged in the wagon, going nowhere in particular, just riding along, is also fine with Christian. Looking back over my shoulder, I see a relaxed, happy child watching the wagon wheels spin, the ants scattering about, or the shadows being cast over the sidewalk in ever-changing patterns as we roll along. When Christian and Amanda were young and both rode in the wagon, Dave and I often found the two snuggled together under a blanket on cool fall mornings or leaning against each other, relaxed and gazing at the clouds in the warm sunshine of summer.

Sledding is a prime activity of Chicago children to help make winter time more tolerable. Christian despised the snow when he was young—too cold, too hard to walk in, too much clothing on body parts that he did not want covered. Dread is the word that best describes our early sledding outings. While his brother and sister squealed with glee over every aspect of sledding, Christian mostly sat in protest at the top of the bunny hill, slumped over at the waist. Repeatedly, we tried to put him on our sled as a passenger, but he met our attempts with outstretched, rigid legs that told us definitively, *No way!* Consequently, one of us, Dave or I, was either stranded at home or stranded at the top of the slope, hopping from foot to foot to keep warm.

Year after year, we exposed Christian to sledding on temperate days and he watched. Then one year, Christian unexpectedly sat on the plastic red toboggan and we shoved him down the hill. It was not steep, and the toboggan was not able to go far, so there was no worry that Christian would hurt himself. We ran down the hill to greet him as he sat immobile on the sled. We waited for his response. Christian rolled over sideways, legs straight, and popped up like a robot ready to do it again. Winter now finds that there isn't a sled, toboggan, or inner tube that he won't ride. Christian often sits peacefully at the bottom of the sledding hill to bask in the glory of the wonderful ride he just enjoyed or to stick his tongue as deeply into the snow as it will go.

Our first really long car ride to Baltimore, when Christian was about seven years old, came with anxiety and worry because we did not know how to keep Christian occupied. Our other two children loaded up a bag full of books, toys, gadgets, and snacks, but what to bring for Christian? Sometimes I caught Christian with his head lazily cocked sideways and a partial smile on his face, creating wonderful images and ideas which we could not see but which kept him happily occupied. It was so funny that we were worried about how to amuse him. Dave and I did not hear the typical "Are we there yet? I'm bored. Can we stop for a while?" I was truly surprised as the hours on the road slid by, and we did not hear a peep from Christian. Perhaps God provides Christian with a fantastic imagination, and although he cannot express it to us, he feels immeasurable contentment and joy during all his rides.

He has filled him with divine spirit.

—Exodus 35:31

LESSON 27

MICROPHONES

Most teens have a long list of increasingly expensive items on their wish lists for birthdays or other present-laden holidays. We ask, "What do you want for your thirteenth birthday, Christian?" A representation of a single word comes: *microphone.* There are five people in our family, plus Grandma, so Christian got five microphones for his birthday. No inkling from Christian of *Is this all? Five microphones? Really?* Christian was as overjoyed with the last microphone as he was with the first. Bounding up the stairs to his room, he immediately began recording his read-aloud story books and songs from the iPad.

We now keep an emergency stash of microphones, in case one breaks, poised upright in the crawlspace, like soldiers ready for action at a moment's notice or maidens-in-waiting ready to share their lives with the one who calls on them. Often we turn our heads, surprised to find a microphone positioned under our lower lip, as Christian waits to catch whatever silly sound or butchered rendition of one of his favorite songs we might provide. I hope in these moments that we're always willing to stop for a moment of silliness to please Christian. With Christian's toy in his hand, we see only gratitude in his eyes for what he truly loves doing—recording on a microphone.

There is great gain in godliness combined with contentment; for we brought nothing into the world, so that we can take nothing out of it; but if we have food and clothing, we will be content with these.

—1 Timothy 6:6–8

FASHION

"Drats. I got the wrong ones again and brought home the pink Little Mermaid swim diapers for Christian," I say, as we head out for the swimming pool. Christian puts the protective garment on without complaint, likely thinking, *Fashion is no problem, Mom. We're going swimming. I'll wear a tutu if I get to go swimming.*

What's cool? What's clean? No matter. Christian loves all his clothes: yard sale items, hand-me-downs, too big, too small—whatever. Stains, rips, tags left on; none of these elicit the complaints I frequently hear from our other two children. No battling over style, quality, or brand.

We do dress Christian in comfortable clothing and articles that are easy to put on because dressing is hard for Christian, and frankly, it saves time and energy. It's pretty cute when Christian stands at the top of the stairs before I've helped him dress, wearing the shirt logo on his back, the underwear outside of his shorts, and his socks ... well, they're just wrong. I'm so proud of his accomplishment that I sometimes don't fix his handiwork, except for the underwear worn on the outside.

Christian is very small for his age. He never quite reached even the lowest red arch on the growth chart at the doctor's office. We believe it's his heart defect (and other medical reasons), coupled with the fact that his gene pool consists mostly of vertically-challenged ancestors; none of his family is considered tall. When Christian stands next to his peers, most of them tower over him by at least a foot. He isn't bothered in the least, and he often gets an extra high-five, especially from the girls, just for being adorable.

Christian is years behind being able to wear his brother's outgrown clothing, but the items are tucked away safely in a box in the crawl space, waiting to be worn. If we count up the amount of money we've saved by Christian's accepting attitude about his clothing and the fact that we don't have to replace items nearly as often as we do for our other children, the benefit is high in the area of fashion.

... and endurance produces character, and character produces hope, and hope does not disappoint us, because God's love has been poured into our hearts.

—Romans 5:4–5

LESSON 29

DIAPERS

The call comes from the top of the stairs, "Maaaaaaaahm!" starting low and ending high, in clear desperation. I'm not sure what I'll find when I reach the top of the stairs. I see children scattering in all directions from Christian's room. As I approach, I smell the reason I was called, as the odor permeates the hallway. To date, I haven't found a way to count joy in the fact that a thirteen-year-old hasn't yet been potty-trained, despite countless seminars and recommended strategies. Diapers are expensive, and Christian's timing doesn't always correspond with opportune moments in our daily activities. It's just not pleasant to change a dirty diaper.

Patience takes practice, and I get frequent lessons on this, particularly when diaper changes aren't convenient or practical. Life's most embarrassing moments for me have often involved Christian not being potty-trained. Our event planning often revolves around whether or not Christian has had a bowel movement, particularly when we go swimming. Double diapering and incessant checking help insure that no accidents happen, so as to avoid our family being shunned or obligating us to change towns. Christian's daily communication sheet from school has a specific line item for whether or not he had a bowel movement that day so that I'm not unpleasantly surprised when I check on him in the bathtub. However, many times the box is checked off and poop happens anyway.

I will have to keep searching for the silver-lined diaper and report back when I'm able to rejoice in this milestone that hasn't yet been reached. We all have habits that we could or should change, and for whatever reason, we don't move forward. Many things hold us back from progressing in certain areas of our lives. Sometimes they're physical, sometimes emotional; sometimes it's just plain stubbornness. Acceptance of things you can't change and mustering strength to deal with difficulties builds character. We will continue to seek ways to help Christian move beyond this limitation in his daily routine. In the meantime, I am reminded that some aspects of life just have to be accepted as they are, and occasional occurrences during the day just stink like dirty diapers.

Clothe yourselves with compassion, kindness, humility, meekness, and patience.

—Colossians 3:12

LESSON 30

CARE

Parents expect to take care of their children. We're the nurturers, running to kiss a boo-boo, applying salve to a cut or scrape, or providing a cold pack as needed. Christian required a lot of care in the first few months of his life and later, from time to time, as we all do. Explanations to Christian about the sniffles, a stomach ache, or a scraped knee could be difficult, and frankly, he didn't appear to want or need an explanation—just a hug or a distraction would usually suffice.

The first time Christian threw up I worried the event would be insurmountable. I feared that he would dread what was to come over and over again and that he would remember the impending heaving as my other children had done. I was wrong, again! When it happened, it happened. Not pleasant for the short time it lasted, but when it was over it was forgotten. Here was Christian, bursting from the bathroom with a smile on his face, as if to say, *Bring on the fun. What can I do now?* Christian's concept of time is different, I think, than most other people, and that is sometimes a blessing, especially when you don't feel well.

When Christian has a cold, he likes to be coddled, so we coddle him. One day when I was sick and lying on the sofa, I found Christian standing over me, just staring, possibly considering my needs. Leaning over, he rubbed my back, alternating rubbing with gentle pats, such as he had received when he was sick and placed his head on my shoulder. Not a word, just an action. If a person coughs in church or another quiet setting, Christian provides a compassionate cough to show his concern. If someone is crying, Christian will sit quietly nearby and sometimes pout along with them in a show of support. His brother and sister have witnessed what a trooper Christian is when he's sick and how quickly he nurtures others when they are sick. I wrongly expected that Christian would only be able to receive, not give care.

Listen to advice and accept instruction, that you may gain wisdom for the future.

—Proverbs 19:20

L E S S O N   3 1

PLAN

So many questions were asked regarding the plan for Christian's future that had never come up in conversations about our other children. What will happen to Christian if we die before him? Are Matt and Amanda responsible for Christian when Dave and I die? Can they be? Do they want to be? Do we think they should be? Who wants to think of these concerns?

These questions are not usually in the minds of new parents as they rejoice over their babies. We certainly didn't discuss these matters after Matt was born. However, with Christian, we realized that guardianship is an important issue for all children, should the unthinkable happen to both parents. And this was especially so, considering one of our children had Down syndrome. So we drafted documents naming guardians for all three of the children to alleviate the burden of our family having to take care of this matter after we pass. We regularly revisit this issue to be sure we have the best possible plan for all of our children, based on our current situation.

The magical age when a child leaves the nest varies, but the plan for Christian is for him to continue to live with us. No one can predict the future, but over these past thirteen years, we are realizing that Christian will likely not develop the skills to allow him to live either independently or in an assisted-housing setting.

While it is wonderful that we will have the pleasure of Christian's company, the financial aspect is a concern for our family.

Soon after Christian's birth, we stumbled upon information that saving is a great idea but not in the traditional way or with the same goals as saving for our other children. We attended a seminar to learn that, in the state of Illinois, Christian may not have more than a limited sum of money to his name at age twenty-one, or he may not qualify for state services.

We might not have thought much about planning and saving had it not been for Christian's special needs calling us to seek counsel from financial experts to put some security in place for our children's futures. To the best of your abilities, envision opportunities for your child, anticipate a bright future, and be willing to revise your plan.

For nothing will be impossible with God.

—1 Luke 1:37

LESSON 32

TOMORROW

I don't know what tomorrow holds for Christian, or any of us for that matter. We may still struggle with some people avoiding us, anticipating that their lives will somehow be burdened because of the compensations we make for Christian. Strangers may continue to shoot uncomfortable glances our way when Christian's behavior steps outside the boundary of typical behavior. My hope is that, by reading this book, anyone who comes into contact with a person with special needs can provide joy with a gentle smile, a welcoming attitude, or an offer to help out in some way. The one receiving the joy just may be you.

If you had asked me when I was single or when I was first married and considering having a family, "Do you want a child with special needs?" my immediate answer would probably have been no. If I could turn the clock back, knowing what I know now, my answer would be a resounding yes! I struggled in Christian's early years and finally embraced the challenges and experiences with hope and positive feelings.

Each of us has a choice in how we view life's challenges. The trials and difficulties will pass, and overcoming challenges may develop qualities in you for your betterment. My hope is that a new parent or a struggling parent of a child with special needs might gain insight from what I have shared. Life is more beautiful, fulfilling, and joyful because Christian is in our family.

So these are my stories, my reality, and my life with Christian. Tomorrow is uncertain. But I am certain that I want to look back on the unremarkable moments in my life with Christian, knowing that I have contributed to making bright and happy memories.

Start your joy today, this very moment. Find joy in the little happenings of daily life with your child. Create your unique, beautiful story of celebration with your child. Make memories today that are beautiful so that you and your family can enjoy them tomorrow.

Let us not become weary in doing good, for at the proper time we will reap a harvest if we do not give up.

—Galatians 6:9

LIFE'S LESSONS FROM A CHILD WITH SPECIAL NEEDS

Today: Make something good happen.

Worry: You can't change how things are, but you can choose how you feel about those things.

Doors: Don't close a door before you know what's on the other side; it might be wonderful.

Locks: Have a sense of humor in life, and find ways around your barriers.

Ears: Appreciate the unique beauty of the human body.

Eyes: Look for goodness inside a person's soul.

Heart: Rejoice in the miracles of medicine.

Mirrors: Let God provide the reality and truth of your reflection. You are loved by Him.

Food: Be creative to live a healthy and happy life.

Donuts: Enjoy the plain pleasures in life.

Play: Turn ordinary into extraordinary.

Bed Time: Simplicity is beautiful.

Words: It's not *how* you communicate; it's *what* you are communicating that's important.

Smiles: The more smiles you give away the more you get back.

Hugs: Give a hug whenever you can; you never know when someone needs one.

God: We are all equal in His sight.

Dad: Be generous with your love and your time.

Brother: Show tenderness every chance you get.

Sister: Be dependable and resourceful.

Stuey: Value all of God's creatures.

Friends: Be accepting and kind to one another.

Neighbors: Laugh together. Offer help to another person when you can.

Teachers: Express in words and actions appreciation for a job well done.

Dance: Inspire yourself to do what you love to do.

Waiting: You can't hasten time, so you might as well enjoy yourself in the moment.

Rides: Be carefree. Pay attention to the small wonders in the world.

Microphones: Appreciate small activities in a huge way.

Fashion: Comfort trumps fashion.

Diapers: Patience takes practice.

Care: Be courageous in caring for yourself and for others.

Plan: Lay out a plan for the future. Change your plan as needed.

Tomorrow: Find peace and joy each day. Precious memories last forever in your heart.

ABOUT THE AUTHOR

Kathleen Murray is the mother of a child with Down syndrome and autism. She holds a doctorate in Communication Sciences and Disorders from Northwestern University and has published several journal articles in her field of study. Dr. Murray enjoys working part-time as a speech-language pathologist. She lives in Naperville, Illinois with her husband, her three children, and her dog.

Author Photo: Scott Pfeiffer
www.pfeiffer-photo.com

Kathleen Murray's email:
drkathleenmurray@wideopenwest.com

ACKNOWLEDGMENTS

The journey of parenthood is somewhat different when you have a child with special needs. A book can connect people in similar situations to each other and help guide them in a positive direction, if they allow it. *Count It All Joy: Life's Lessons from a Child with Special Needs* was difficult for me to write in many ways. It was painful for me to acknowledge my negative feelings toward Christian and my life circumstances in the early years with him. However, I am truly grateful to God for helping me find abundant joy, as He intended, and for giving me the strength to share my story.

My life would have taken an entirely different path had I not met my husband, Dave, who showed me what is truly valuable—loving and caring for each other and for our children. His devotion to me during the writing and repeated editing of this book is greatly appreciated. My children, Matt and Amanda, are precious blessings to me and to Christian. Words cannot express the deep love I have for them.

My wholehearted gratitude goes to my mom, Gloria Goldstraw, for her love, invaluable comments, ongoing support, and endless believing.

Very special appreciation also to Lynn Woodman, for her effort and contributions that helped me convey my ideas more clearly.

I would also like to thank the many professors at Towson State University and Northwestern University who modeled hard work and dedication toward achieving life's goals.

My treasured family and friends and valued colleagues have been generous with their thoughts, guidance, and encouragement.

And, most deeply, much love to Christian, my sweet angel, who reminds me every day of the importance of unconditional love and the creation of beautiful memories.

For the Lord does not see as mortals see; they look on the outward appearance, but the Lord looks on the heart.

—1 Samuel 16:7

MORE FROM THE AUTHOR

Publications:

Murray, K. A. and Perkins, N. L. "Ready, Set, Action: Understanding and Using Verbs." Copyright © 2004 by Murray and Perkins. Library of Congress Catalog Card Number: TXu 1-191-959.

Murray, K. A., Larson, C. R., and Logemann, J. A. "Electromyographic response of the labial muscles during normal liquid swallows using a spoon, a straw, and a cup." *Dysphagia*, 13 (1998): 160–166.

Murray, K. A. and Brzozowski, L. A. "Swallowing in patients with tracheotomies." *AACN Clinical Issues*, 9(3) (1998): 416–426.

Weinrich, M., McCall, D. M., Shoosmith, L. A., Thomas, K., Katzenberger (Murray), K. A., and Weber, C. A. "Locative prepositional phrases in severe aphasia." *Brain and Language*, 45 (1993): 21–45.

United States Patent:

Murray, Kathy. 1997. Therapeutic Drinking Straw Machine. US
Patent 5,662,268, filed June 15, 1995, and issued September
2, 1997.

NOTES

CPSIA information can be obtained at www.ICGtesting.com
Printed in the USA
BVOW08s0057091015

421729BV00001B/8/P